Fact Finders®

DISGUSTING JOBS
ON THE AMERICAN
FRONTIER

THE DOWN AND DIRTY DETAILS

BY ANITA YASUDA

Content Consultant:
James E. Crisp, Professor, Department of History,
North Carolina State University

CAPSTONE PRESS
a capstone imprint

Fact Finders Books are published by Capstone Press,
1710 Roe Crest Drive, North Mankato, Minnesota 56003
www.mycapstone.com

Library of Congress Cataloging-in-Publication Data
Names: Yasuda, Anita, author.
Title: Disgusting jobs on the American frontier : the down and dirty details / by Anita Yasuda.
Description: North Mankato, Minnesota : Capstone Press, 2018. | Series: Fact finders. Disgusting jobs in history
| Includes bibliographical references and index. | Audience: Age 8-10. | Audience: Grade 4 to 6.
Identifiers: LCCN 2017038580 (print) | LCCN 2017039104 (ebook) | ISBN 9781543503722 (eBook PDF) | ISBN
9781543503685 (hardcover)
Subjects: LCSH: Frontier and pioneer life—West (U.S.) —Juvenile literature. | West (U.S.)—Social life and
customs—Juvenile literature.
Classification: LCC F591 (ebook) | LCC F591 .Y37 2018 (print) | DDC 978—dc23
LC record available at https://lccn.loc.gov/2017038580

Editorial Credits
Editor: Alyssa Krekelberg
Designer: Maggie Villaume
Production specialist: Laura Manthe

Photo Credits
Alamy: Corey Hochachka/Design Pics Inc, 11, Michal Besser, 20, Science History Images, 6–7, The Natural
History Museum, 26; iStockphoto: IndyEdge, 8, jmoor17, 14, kaczor58, 28, LifeJourneys, 27, phillipimage,
24–25, stanley45, 8–9; Shutterstock Images: Erni, cover (top right), Everett Historical, cover (bottom), 13,
Fitzthum Photography, 21, iravgustin, 22, Ivan Smuk, 5 (top), Luchenko Yana, 5 (map background), Maen
Zayyad, 15, Margaret M Stewart, cover (top left), Nick Starichenko, 23, schankz, 19, welcomia, 18–19 (bottom),
Yossawat fangseing, 18 (top), Zack Frank, 5 (bottom); SuperStock: Joseph Barnell, 16–17

Design Elements: iStockphoto, Shutterstock Images, and Red Line Editorial

Printed and bound in Canada.
010800S18

TABLE OF CONTENTS

ADVENTURE

The days of the far–western American frontier were a time of great growth. Thousands of people moved west of the Mississippi River. They were eager for new lives out west, but life was rough. Many people struggled to build new lives on the frontier. They worked long hours year-round just to survive. In some areas, there was little clean water or food. Without these essentials people became ill.

Pioneer families frequently discovered maggots creeping into their food. Millions of whizzing insects followed their every step. Trappers scraped the flesh and fat from animals such as beavers, elk, bears, and deer. Cowboys drove cattle over long, dusty trails. Miners also moved west. They lived in dirt and filth, and fleas fed on their skin.

1822

American fur companies begin advertising for men to work as trappers. Trappers move out west looking for valuable animal skins.

1841

The first group of settlers heads west across the Rocky Mountains. Thousands more settlers follow looking for land to farm. Accidents and deadly diseases kill as many as 65,000 people over the next 25 years.

JANUARY 24, 1848

Gold is discovered in California. Gold miners rush west in a search for quick riches.

OCTOBER 26, 1863

Railroad workers begin construction of the Transcontinental Railroad. The railroad will join the East Coast to the West Coast of the United States.

1867

Cowboys begin herding cattle along the Chisholm Trail from Texas to Kansas in the first cattle drive. By the late 1800s, more than six million cattle will be herded out of Texas.

MAY 10, 1869

Railroad workers lay thousands of miles of track to complete the Transcontinental Railroad.

1871

The largest cattle drive begins. Cowboys herd 700,000 longhorns from Texas to Kansas.

OREGON TRAIL

Fur trappers came to Fort Hall to sell the furs that they scraped from dead animals.

OREGON

IDAHO

FORT BOISE

FORT HALL

WYOMING

FORT LARAMIE

FORT BRIDGER

NEBRASKA

In the 1800s, the Oregon Trail helped bring settlers west. They stopped at forts to rest and get supplies.

KANSAS

MISSOURI

Thousands of tired, dirty travelers on their way to Oregon and California stopped at Fort Laramie.

CHAPTER ONE

TERRIBLE TRAPPERS

In the warm weather, trappers were tormented by masses of biting insects. Nasty black flies feasted on their skin and mosquitoes stuck to their hands and faces. The bugs landed on their eyes and flew into their noses. Men smeared bear fat and skunk urine on their skin. They hoped this would keep the pests away.

FOUL FACT

Fur trappers ate whatever they could hunt or shoot. On expeditions that went terribly wrong, men went days without food or water.

Trappers needed to stay healthy. It took strength to trap animals. To lure a beaver, trappers made a liquid that would attract the animal. They squeezed the sacs from under the beaver's bottom. Brown goo that looked like molasses would come out. They mixed the goo with spices and spread it in traps. After a beaver was caught, men peeled off its hide. They scraped it clean of every lump of fat and saved the fur.

beaver trap

"a pair of scissors and cut off [the trapper's] hair. Then, I began
t job of dressing wounds. I saw that the bear had taken nearly all
ead in its huge mouth. It had bitten close to his left eye on one
d close to his right ear on the other. It had laid the skull bare near
wn. There was a white streak where the bear's teeth had passed.
his ears was torn from his head out to outer rim."

—*James Clyman, trapper*, 1824

Trappers had many uses for the beaver goo. They used it as a treatment for **frostbite** and cuts. The goo was smeared over open wounds. It mixed with the trapper's blood, but it did not help to heal the wound. If a wound got infected, blood and pus would ooze out of the injury.

Trappers met yearly to trade furs for supplies such as traps, knives, and guns. At trading posts, rats lurked in every corner. There was no way to keep them out. These rodents ate the trappers' food. They left their shiny, black poop behind. Some people killed the rats, but others made a meal of them.

frostbite — when tissue is damaged from very cold temperatures

Trading posts were created so
goods such as furs could be sol

CHAPTER TWO

MISERABLE MINERS

Beginning in 1848, thousands of people rushed west. Gold had been discovered in California, and many people hoped to use this opportunity to get rich. Men toiled in dirt and in icy streams, searching for gold buried in the gravel and sand. Their hands were raw and covered with bubbling blisters from using a pick day after day. If a blister popped, yellow pus spilled out.

Miners' backs ached from the nonstop scraping and lifting of dirt. A man might heave 800 buckets of dirt a day and find nothing. Rocks could crush miners' fingers and feet. If they lost their footing down a steep bank, their ankles could break.

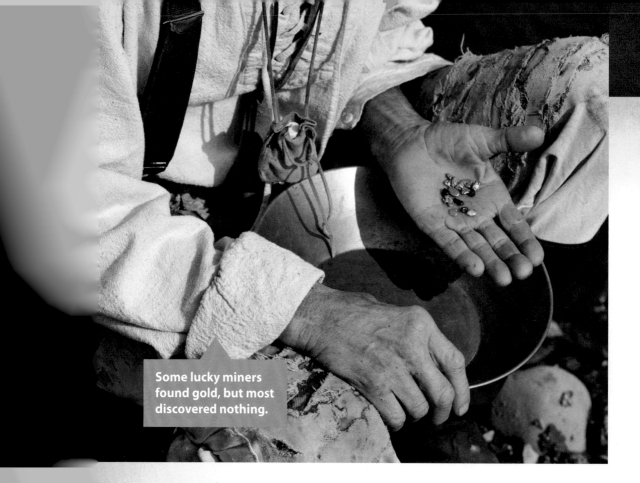

Some lucky miners found gold, but most discovered nothing.

After a long, hard day of digging, miners came home to their camps. Animal poop and human waste lay in the mud surrounding them. The smell of rot swept through the camps.

Miners were coated in sweat and mud. Little bugs lived all over their bodies. Miners could not rid themselves of lice and fleas that nested in their long, tangled hair.

They bathed in muddy streams, and they pounded and scrubbed their clothes. No matter what they did, dirt clung to them and washing did nothing to get rid of the fleas.

animal poop

RAILROAD WORKERS

In 1863 workers began laying the tracks for a railroad. The railroad would link the country from coast to coast. Thousands of Chinese workers laid tracks in the Sierra Nevada mountain range in California. They spent most of their time underground like moles. In coffin-like tunnels, they drilled and dug with only hammers and hand drills.

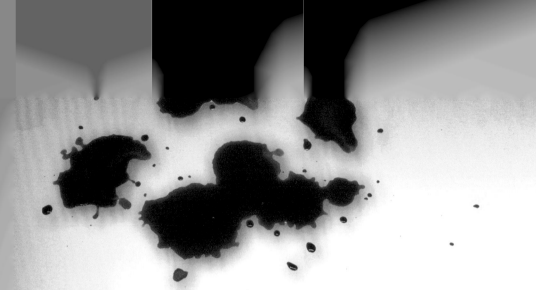

With each blow of the pick, dust spit into the air. It coated their mouths and noses and scarred their lungs. After a while, a person began to spit up blood.

The groans and shrieks of men echoed through the air as they worked. Some lost fingers and hands. Others died from the dangerous work. A roar like thunder meant that land had given in. Mining and tunneling weakened the land and made it unstable. Huge boulders fell, crushing men and entire camps.

FOUL FACT

Many railroad workers drank contaminated water from puddles and barrels. Because of this, many got a disease called **dysentery**.

dysentery — an infection caused by dirty water that leads to diarrhea and blood loss

SORRY SODBUSTERS

On the plains, wood was scarce. So pioneers built homes with strips of muddy **sod**. Mice and rats nested in the walls. Snakes slithered between the cracks. When it rained, muddy rivers drizzled down walls.

Pioneer women made candles with fat from butchered pigs or cows. It was called **tallow**. They collected the fat all year long in jars.

tallow

sod — a section of land cut or torn from the surface of grassland, containing dirt and roots of grass

tallow — pure fat made from boiled animal fat

soaps

To make soap, women mixed tallow with a brown ooze called **lye**. The lye was added to a hot pot with scraps of fat and other food drippings. The boiling pot gurgled. It belched up eye-watering fumes. It was stirred for hours until the slimy liquid thickened into soap.

Pioneer families struggled to grow enough food to eat. Swarms of grasshoppers ate the crops down to the roots.

lye — a substance made by soaking ashes and wood in water; used in making detergents and soap

FOUL FACT

Pioneers could not always find firewood because there were so few trees on the plains. They had to collect heaps of **bison** poop to burn. The poop burned well, and the pioneers could cook over it, but it smelled terrible.

A few people tried eating the insects in broths and stews, but most just wanted to rid their farms of them.

Some pioneers walked miles to fetch drinking water. It came from muddy streams or ditches. Grasshoppers gathered in the water and died. Their bodies rotted on the surface of the water. People brushed away the bugs and drank it. This could sometimes lead to diseases.

bison — an ox-like animal with long, shaggy hair

ROTTEN WRANGLERS

Keeping cattle healthy kept cowboys busy. Flies laid shiny, white eggs in animals' open sores. One fly could lay up to 300 eggs. The eggs became inch-long **screwworms**. The worms ate away the animal's flesh and could kill it. If cowboys didn't have medicine for the animals, they packed the wound with dried cow poop, or they tried pouring liquid on the cut.

screwworms — fly larvae or maggots that feed on warm-blooded animals

Screwworms dig deep into the animal's tissue.

a cattle drive

This would bring the squirming worms to the surface. It was up to cowboys to pull out each worm.

On the trail, cowboys had to be ready for all sorts of risks. Every man dreaded a **stampede**. Cattle are easily frightened. A strange smell, lightning, thunder, or even a sneeze could cause a herd to bolt. Sometimes, cowboys sewed shut the eyes of the animals that had started the stampede. The sewing thread slowly rotted away.

DEAR DIARY

"If a storm came and the cattle started running—you'd hear that low rumbling noise along the ground. The men on herd wouldn't need to come in and tell you. You'd know. Then, you'd jump for your horse and get out there in the lead. Trying to head them . . . before they scattered. . . . It was riding at a dead run in the dark. With cut banks and prairie dog holes all around you, not knowing if the next jump would land you in a shallow grave."

—*E. C. Abbott, cowboy,* 1879

After hours in the saddle under the sun, cowboys were hungry. They ate a simple diet of beans and pork. Their biscuits were alive with wormy maggots. But they ate them anyway.

NEW OPPORTUNITIES

After the railroad was completed in 1869, it was easier for people to move west. The west became wealthier as towns grew. A number of men and women worked as doctors, nurses, and lawyers. People built mills and printed newspapers. Some towns had general stores, banks, and **saloons**. Larger towns hired sheriffs and deputies.

Young women with an education were also encouraged to come west. Pioneers had large families and they needed teachers for the growing number of children. These women taught in any available space. Only some towns had money to build a school.

New achievements in technology and manufacturing meant that new types of jobs were created. Many Americans left farms for jobs in factories. As job opportunities grew, so did the variety of smelly, dirty, and disgusting jobs.

saloons — buildings where alcoholic drinks are sold

GLOSSARY

bison (BY-son) — an ox-like animal with long, shaggy hair

dysentery (DISS-in-tair-ee) — an infection caused by dirty water that leads to diarrhea and blood loss

frostbite (FRAWST-bite) — when tissue is damaged from very cold temperatures

lye (LIE) — a substance made by soaking ashes and wood in water; used in making detergents and soap

saloons (suh-LOONZ) — buildings where alcoholic drinks are sold

screwworms (SKROO-wurmz) — fly larvae or maggots that feed on warm-blooded animals

sod (SAHD) — a section of land cut or torn from the surface of grassland, containing dirt and roots of grass

stampede (stam-PEED) — when a group of frightened animals suddenly begins running

tallow (TA-loh) — pure fat made from boiled animal fat

READ MORE

Hester, Sallie. *Diary of Sallie Hester: A Covered Wagon Girl*. North Mankato, Minn.: Capstone Press, 2014.

Kravitz, Danny. *Surviving the Journey: The Story of the Oregon Trail*. North Mankato, Minn.: Capstone Press, 2015.

Musolf, Nell. *The Split History of Westward Expansion in the United States: American Indian Perspective*. North Mankato, Minn.: Compass Point, 2013.

INTERNET SITES

Use FactHound to find Internet sites related to this book.

Visit *www.facthound.com*

Type in this code: 9781543503685

CRITICAL THINKING QUESTIONS

1. If you could go back in time, which of the disgusting jobs described in this book would you try?

2. How does the information graphic on page 5 help you to understand the difficulty of the journey to the west?

3. Why do you think people took these disgusting and dangerous jobs on the far-western American frontier?

INDEX

ABOUT THE AUTHOR

Anita Yasuda is the author of many books for young readers. Her children's book *Explore Simple Machines!* won the Society of School Librarians International Honor Book Award for science books, grades K–6 in 2012. Anita is a history buff who visits historical sites across North America. Anita lives with her family in California.